Congressional
Research
Service

The Federal Employees' Compensation Act (FECA): Workers' Compensation for Federal Employees

Scott Szymendera
Analyst in Disability Policy

November 7, 2012

Congressional Research Service

7-5700

www.crs.gov

R42107

Summary

The Federal Employees' Compensation Act (FECA) is the workers' compensation program for federal employees. Like all workers' compensation programs, FECA pays disability, survivors, and medical benefits, without fault, to employees who are injured or become ill in the course of their federal employment and the survivors of employees killed on the job. The FECA program is administered by the Department of Labor (DOL) and the costs of benefits are paid by each employee's host agency. Employees of the U.S. Postal Service (USPS) currently comprise the largest group of FECA beneficiaries and are responsible for the largest share of FECA benefits.

The modern FECA program can trace its roots to 1916 but has not been significantly amended since 1974. Today, the FECA program pays a basic disability benefit equal to two-thirds of an injured worker's pre-disability wage, which rises to 75% of the pre-disability wage if the worker has any dependents. Benefits continue for the duration of disability or the life of the beneficiary and in cases of traumatic injuries, beneficiaries can receive a continuation of their full pay for the first 45 days. Persons with specific permanent partial disabilities, such as the loss of a limb, are entitled to disability benefits for a set number weeks provided by schedules set by statute and regulation. All medical costs associated with covered conditions are provided by the FECA program without any copayments, cost-sharing, or use of private insurance by the beneficiaries. The survivors of employees killed on the job are entitled to cash benefits based on the worker's wages and a modest benefit for funeral costs. Beneficiaries are also entitled to vocational rehabilitation services to assist them in returning to work.

In the 112th Congress, several committees have held hearings on the FECA program. These hearings have identified several key policy issues facing the program, including the disproportionate share of claims and program costs attributed to postal workers, the payment of FECA benefits after retirement age, the overall generosity of FECA disability benefits as compared with those offered by the states, and the administration of the FECA program.

To address some of these policy issues, committees in the House and Senate passed legislation that would make changes to the FECA program. In the House, H.R. 2309 would set financial conditions under which the USPS would be required to create a new workers' compensation system for its employees. Additional bills, H.R. 2465, passed by the House, and S. 1789, would make changes to the FECA program for all federal employees with the Senate legislation reducing benefit levels for beneficiaries over retirement age and eliminating augmented compensation for dependents.

This report will be updated to reflect major legislative activity.

Contents

Tables

Appendixes

Contacts

Introduction

The Federal Employees' Compensation Act (FECA) is the workers' compensation system for federal employees. Every civilian employee of the federal government, including employees of the legislative and judicial branches, is covered by FECA, as are several other groups, including federal jurors and Peace Corps volunteers. In FY2009, the FECA program paid out more than $2.7 billion in benefits, including $1.8 billion in disability benefits, $847 million in medical benefits, and $138 million in benefits to the survivors of federal employees killed on the job.[1] In FY2009, administrative expenses made up 4.9% of total program costs.[2]

Legislative History of FECA

The FECA program has its origins in a law from the late 1800s that covered only the employees of a federal agency that has long since ceased to exist on its own. The modern FECA system has its roots in legislation enacted in 1916; many of the basic provisions of this original law, such as the basic rate of compensation, are still in effect today. Congress passed major amendments to the 1916 legislation in 1949, 1960, 1966, and most recently in 1974. Although these amendments made significant changes to the FECA program, the basic framework of the program endures as does the overall intent of Congress through the years to maintain a workers' compensation system for federal employees that is in line with the basic principles that have governed workers' compensation in this country for a century.

Limited Workers' Compensation for the United States Life Saving Service and Other Hazardous Federal Occupations

The first workers' compensation law for federal employees was enacted in 1882 and provided up to two years of salary to any member of the federal United States Life Saving Service disabled in the line of duty and two years of salary to his or her survivors in case of a line of duty death.[3] In 1908, Congress passed a more comprehensive workers' compensation law for federal employees engaged in certain hazardous occupations, such as laborers at federal manufacturing facilities and arsenals or workers at the construction of the Panama Canal. This law provided workers with up to one year of salary, after a 15-day waiting period, if disabled due to an employment-related injury and their survivors with up to a year of salary in case of death.

The 1882 and 1908 federal workers' compensation laws did not provide universal coverage for all federal employees. It is estimated that only one-fourth of the federal workforce was covered by the 1908 law, and the law was clearly designed only to provide coverage for what were seen to be the most hazardous jobs in the civil service.[4] President Theodore Roosevelt recognized this

---

[1] Department of Labor, Office of Workers' Compensation Programs, *Annual Report to Congress: FY2009*, Washington, DC, April 27, 2011, p. 7.

[2] Ibid, p. 15.

[3] Act of May 4, 1882, ch. 117, 22 Stat. 55 (1882). In 1915 the United States Life Saving Service was merged with the Revenue Cutter Service to form the United States Coast Guard.

[4] Willis J. Nordlund, "The Federal Employees' Compensation Act," *Monthly Labor Review*, September 1991, p. 5. (Hereafter cited as Nordlund 1991.)

shortcoming of the law he would eventually sign. Before the 1908 law's passage, he called on Congress to pass a workers' compensation bill that would cover "all employees injured in the government service" and stated that the lack of such a comprehensive workers' compensation law was "a matter of humiliation to the nation."[5]

In addition to only covering a small portion of the federal workforce, the 1882 and 1908 laws did not provide for medical benefits for disabled workers, and the 1908 law only applied in cases of disability or death arising from injuries and not illnesses.

The Federal Employees' Compensation Act of 1916

President Woodrow Wilson signed the Federal Employees' Compensation Act, P.L. 64-267, into law on September 7, 1916, and in so doing extended the protections of the modern workers' compensation system to nearly all federal employees. This original FECA law remains the basis for the workers' compensation system for the federal civil service.

The FECA law provided coverage for nearly all civilian employees of the federal government injured or killed in line of duty. Coverage was not provided for occupational illnesses.[6] The law provided full medical coverage for covered injuries provided by government physicians and hospitals or private medical services selected by the government. Disability compensation was provided, after a three-day waiting period, at a rate of two-thirds of the worker's wage for total disability, with adjustments for partial disabilities. Disability benefits were subject to minimum and maximum levels specified in the law and neither benefits nor these levels were subject to any cost-of-living or other annual adjustments. The survivors of an employee killed on the job were entitled to cash benefits based on the worker's wage and were also entitled to a benefit to help offset funeral costs.

The 1916 legislation created the Federal Employees' Compensation Commission, with three members appointed by the President with the advice and consent of the Senate, to administer the FECA program. Benefit and administrative costs associated with the program were paid out of the Employees' Compensation Fund created by the law and financed with permanently authorized appropriations.

Congressional Intent

Bringing the Federal System in Line with the States

Congress had several clear intentions when drafting the FECA program in 1916. One such intention was to bring the protections offered to federal employees in line with those being offered by a majority of the states at the time, with the House Judiciary Committee reporting that such state laws were "working with most excellent results."[7] In addition, the committee reported

---

[5] U.S. Congress, House Committee on Education and Labor, Subcommittee on Safety and Compensation, *Amendments to Federal Employees' Compensation Act*, hearings on H.R. 1196 and other bills to amend the Federal Employees' Compensation Act, 86th Cong., 2nd sess., February 10, 23, 24 and March 8, 23, 24, 1960 (Washington: GPO, 1960), p. 124.

[6] Coverage for occupational illnesses was added to the FECA program in 1924 by P.L. 68-195.

[7] U.S. Congress, House Committee on the Judiciary, *Compensation of Government Employees Suffering Injuries While* (continued...)

that the schedule of compensation for disability in FECA was "in line with the best precedents found in State compensation acts," especially those in Massachusetts, New York, and Ohio.[8]

Providing Coverage to all Federal Employees

An additional intention of Congress was to provide workers' compensation coverage to all federal employees regardless of occupation, thus correcting what was seen as a shortcoming of the 1908 act. The House Judiciary Committee's report on the 1916 FECA legislation criticizes the limited coverage of the 1908 law and states,

> The present law, in denying compensation to an injured employee if his occupation was not "hazardous" goes counter to the theory on which all compensation acts are based, viz, that the industry shall bear the burden of injuries caused by it.[9]

This criticism of the limited coverage provided by the 1908 act, and the intention of the FECA legislation to correct this shortcoming, was echoed by the FECA legislation's sponsor in the Senate, Senator George Sutherland. Senator Sutherland, in a Senate Judiciary Committee hearing on the legislation, stated,

> The theory upon which compensation laws are drawn is that you are to compensate for the injury, not for the risk that the man ran in bringing about the injury; and under modern thought there is no logical reason for making distinction between what is hazardous and non-hazardous employment.[10]

Senator Sutherland reinforced his point with a rather graphic example stating "the clerk who has his leg cut off in his work about a store is just as effectively deprived of his leg as if it was cut off by a machine."[11]

Major FECA Amendments

Congress has passed major amendments to the FECA program in 1949, 1960, 1966, and most recently in 1974.

1949 Amendments

The Federal Employees' Compensation Act Amendments of 1949, P.L. 81-357, brought about the first set of significant changes to the FECA program since its inception in 1916. The 1949 amendments, in the words of the House Committee on Education and Labor, sought to

---

(...continued)

on Duty, report to accompany H.R. 15316, 64th Cong., 2nd sess., May 11, 1916, H. Rept. 64-678 (Washington: GPO, 1916), p. 7.

[8] Ibid., p. 9.

[9] Ibid., p. 8.

[10] U.S. Congress, Senate Committee on the Judiciary, *Accident Compensation to Government Employees*, hearing on S. 2846, 64th Cong., 1st sess., February 26, 1916 (Washington: GPO, 1916), p. 27.

[11] Ibid.

"modernize and liberalize" the FECA program, which, according to the Senate Committee on Labor and Public Welfare, provided "only illusory security for most workers or their families."[12]

Increased FECA Coverage

The 1949 amendments expanded the scope of workers covered by the FECA program to include those classified as "officers" of the United States. The amendments also doubled the maximum disability benefit level, thus providing for a replacement of a larger portion of federal employee pay.

In addition to better meeting the goal of universal coverage of all employees, the inclusion of federal government officers was intended to provide FECA protections to previously excluded employees, such as Foreign Service Officers, who may serve in dangerous overseas areas. The increase in the maximum benefit level was necessary since, at the time, it was estimated by the Department of Labor (DOL) that 90% of FECA cases involved workers with wages that were essentially not covered by the program because of the low maximum benefit level.[13]

Increased FECA Benefits

Several provisions of the 1949 amendments effectively increased FECA benefits for workers and their survivors. The three-day waiting period for FECA disability compensation was eliminated in cases of disability lasting more than 21 days. A schedule of benefits for permanent partial disabilities was created for the first time, which permitted partial disability benefits to be paid without regard to actual impairment or wage loss. The elimination of the waiting period and creation of a benefits schedule were intended to bring the FECA program in line with state workers' compensation programs and the federal Longshore and Harbor Workers' Compensation Act program.[14]

The 1949 amendments provided for augmented compensation, in the amount of 8.33% of a workers' pre-disability wage, in cases in which an injured worker had at least one dependent. This augmented compensation, along with the standard compensation rate of two-thirds of the workers' wage, brought the level of FECA benefits for workers with dependents up to the current level of 75% of the worker's pre-disability wage. The benefit level for survivors was similarly increased. The intent of the augmented-compensation provision was to better insure that disabled workers and the survivors of workers killed on the job could provide economically for their dependents. The two-thirds benefit level for dependents was criticized by the House and Senate committees that reported the bill as "not sufficient as to ensure reasonable economic security to a

---

[12] U.S. Congress, House Committee on Education and Labor, *Amendments to Federal Employees' Compensation Act*, report to accompany H.R. 3141, 81st Cong., 1st sess., June 6, 1949, H. Rept. 81-729 (Washington: GPO, 1949), p. 23, hereafter cited as H.Rept. 81-729; and U.S. Congress, Senate Labor and Public Welfare, *Amendments to Federal Employees' Compensation Act*, report to accompany H.R. 3141, 81st Cong., 1st sess., August 4, 1949, S.Rept. 81-836 (Washington: GPO, 1949), p. 29, hereafter cited as S.Rept. 81-836.

[13] Nordlund 1991, p. 10.

[14] The Longshore and Harbor Workers' Compensation Act Program was created in 1927. For additional information on the Longshore and Harbor Workers' Compensation Act, see CRS Report R41506, *The Longshore and Harbor Workers' Compensation Act (LHWCA): Overview of Workers' Compensation for Certain Private-Sector Maritime Workers*, by Scott Szymendera.

family of a deceased worker where there is a large family."[15] Similar concerns over the adequacy of the two-thirds benefit level were expressed at a House Committee on Education and Labor hearing on the 1949 amendments.[16]

Reduced Benefits at Age 70

Although the 1949 amendments generally increased the level of FECA benefits, the amendments also required the FECA administrator to review the amount of compensation paid to any person aged 70 or older. The administrator was provided the authority to reduce the amount of such benefits if it was determined that the worker's wage-earning capacity had been reduced because of age, independent of his or her disability. This provision was opposed by several representatives from federal employee organizations who testified before the House Education and Labor Committee. They testified that such a provision was inconsistent with the mandatory federal employee retirement age of 70, in place at the time, and could cause undue hardships to workers who, because of their disabilities, had not been able to reach their full-earning potential or who had reduced pensions because of many years of limited or no earnings.[17]

Provisions for Vocational Rehabilitation

The 1949 amendments permitted the FECA program administrator to send beneficiaries to receive vocational rehabilitation services at the government's expense. The amendments also created a special supplemental benefit for workers participating in vocational rehabilitation programs. These provisions were intended to improve the return-to-work prospects of FECA claimants, which, it was thought, would ultimately benefit both the employee through a return to earning wages and the government through a reduction in FECA-benefit costs.[18]

The Exclusive Remedy Rule

The 1949 amendments established that the FECA program would be the exclusive remedy against the federal government for federal workers with employment-related injuries, illnesses, and deaths. This provision prohibited employees from seeking to recover economic or non-economic damages from the government for injuries, illnesses, and deaths covered by FECA and brought the FECA program in line with one of the general principles of workers' compensation that was already written into the workers' compensation laws in the states.

When the FECA program was created, an exclusive remedy rule was seen as unnecessary because of the general prohibition against suits against the federal government. However, by 1949, three factors had combined to result in significant numbers of federal employees choosing to bring lawsuits against the federal government rather than file for FECA benefits. First, the passage after 1916 of laws, such as the Federal Tort Claims Act, which permitted some suits against the

---

[15] H.Rept. 81-279, p. 11; and S.Rept. 81-836, p. 20.

[16] U.S. Congress, House Committee on Education and Labor, Special Subcommittee, *Federal Employees' Compensation Act Amendments of 1949*, hearing on H.R. 3191 and companion bills, 81st Cong., 1st sess., April 11-13 and May 2, 1949.

[17] Ibid.

[18] H.Rept. 81-279, p. 16; and S.Rept. 81-836, p. 24.

government.[19] Second, some injuries to federal employees occurred while they worked for government corporations subject to lawsuits. Finally, because FECA benefits are limited by statute to partial wage replacement and medical benefits, employees felt that they could secure greater financial benefits from the courts than from the FECA program.[20]

1960 Amendments

The Chargeback Process

The Federal Employees' Compensation Act Amendments of 1960, P.L. 86-767, created the chargeback process in which the Secretary of Labor is required to bill each federal agency for the costs of FECA benefits provided to their employees in the previous fiscal year so that these agencies may reimburse the Employees' Compensation Fund. In addition, these amendments required that government corporations also pay their "fair share" of FECA administrative costs to the government. The chargeback process was intended by Congress to "further the promotion of safety" among federal agencies by making the agencies ultimately responsible for the costs of injuries, illnesses, and deaths of their employees.[21]

1966 Amendments

The Federal Employees' Compensation Act Amendments of 1966, P.L. 89-488, made two significant changes to the FECA program. These changes continue to be in effect today.

Use of the GS Scale to Set Minimum and Maximum Benefit Levels

Prior to the enactment of the 1966 amendments, the maximum and minimum levels of FECA benefits were set by statute and not subject to any automatic adjustments. In 1966, FECA benefits were still subject to levels enacted as part of the 1949 amendments. According to the Senate Committee on Labor and Public Welfare, the statutory maximum provided for full benefits for more than 99% of claimants in 1949, but only 85% of claimants by 1966.[22] To address the difficulty inherent in using statutory changes to keep pace with the growth in federal employees' wages, the 1966 amendments provide for use of the general schedule (GS) scale as the basis for the maximum and minimum FECA benefit levels with the maximum level set at 75% of the highest rate of basic pay at the GS-15 level and the minimum level set at 75% of the lowest rate of basic pay at the GS-2 level.

---

[19] For additional information on the Federal Tort Claims Act, see CRS Report 95-717, *Federal Tort Claims Act (FTCA)*, by Vivian S. Chu.

[20] H.Rept. 81-279, p. 14; and S.Rept. 81-836, p. 23.

[21] U.S. Congress, House Committee on Education and Labor, *Federal Employees' Compensation Act Amendments of 1960*, report to accompany H.R. 12383, 86th Cong., 2nd sess., June 2, 1960, H.Rept. 86-1743 (Washington: GPO, 1960), p. 3; and U.S. Congress, Senate Committee on Labor and Public Welfare, *Federal Employees' Compensation Act Amendments of 1960*, report to accompany H.R. 12383, 86th Cong., 2nd sess., August 27, 1960, S.Rept. 86-1924 (Washington: GPO, 1960), p. 3.

[22] U.S. Congress, Senate Committee on Labor and Public Welfare, *Federal Employees' Compensation Act Amendments of 1966*, report to accompany H.R. 10721, 89th Cong., 2nd sess., June 16, 1966, S.Rept. 89-1285, p. 3.

Cost-of-Living Adjustment for Benefits

The 1966 amendments provided for an annual cost-of-living adjustment for FECA benefits.[23] This annual adjustment is a unique feature of the FECA program not found in other workers' compensation systems.

1974 Amendments

The Federal Employees' Compensation Act Amendments of 1974, P.L. 93-416, made three major changes to the FECA program. These three changes remain key elements of the program today.

Continuation of Pay

The 1974 amendments provided for up to 45 days of continuation of pay from a worker's employing agency in cases of traumatic injuries covered by FECA. During this period, an injured employee may receive his or her full pay rather than FECA compensation. Because continuation of pay is considered income rather than a benefit, it is subject to the federal income tax and is reduced by all standard payroll deductions.

Congress felt that 45 days of continuation of pay were needed because of the time it often took for FECA claims to be processed and compensation benefits to begin. In its report on the 1974 amendments, the Senate Committee on Labor and Public Welfare cited a General Accounting Office report that stated that the average processing time for FECA claims was between 49 and 70 days, a delay that the committee found "creates economic hardship on the injured employee and his or her family and causes difficult administrative problems for the Secretary of Labor and the employing agencies."[24]

Employee Choice of Physician

The 1974 amendments authorized employees to select their own treating physicians rather than use doctors employed or selected by the federal government. The right of employees to have free choice over who provides their medical care was one of the recommendations of the National Commission on State Workmen's Compensation Laws in 1972; this provision brought the FECA program in line with that recommendation as well as some other workers' compensation systems.

Elimination of Reduced Benefits After Age 70

The 1974 amendments removed the provision, enacted as part of the 1949 amendments, requiring that FECA benefits be reviewed and permitting FECA benefits to be reduced after a claimant reached the age of 70 to account for the reduced earning capacity that may come with age

---

[23] The current cost-of-living adjustment is made each year on March 1 and is based on changes in the Consumer Price Index for Urban Wage Earners and Clerical Workers (CPI-W; all items-United States city average) as measured in December of each year.

[24] U.S. Congress, Senate Committee on Labor and Public Welfare, *Federal Employees' Compensation Act of 1970*, report to accompany H.R. 13871, 93rd Cong., 2nd sess., August 8, 1974, S.Rept. 93-1081 (Washington: GPO, 1974), pp. 3-4, hereafter cited as S.Rept. 93-1081; and U.S. General Accounting Office, *Need for a Faster Way to Pay Compensation Claims to Disabled Federal Employees*, B-157593, November 21, 1973, p. 1.

independent of any disability. In its report on the 1974 amendments, the Senate Committee on Labor and Public Welfare provided the following justification for eliminating the reduced benefit provision:

> The Committee finds that such a review places an unnecessary burden on both the employees receiving compensation and the Secretary. Further, the fact that an employee reaches 70 has no bearing on his or her entitlement to benefits and is considered discriminatory in the Committee's opinion.[25]

Recent FECA Amendments

There have been no major amendments to the FECA program since 1974. However, the 109th and 110th Congresses did make changes to FECA that partially address two of the issues currently facing the program.

Change to the FECA Waiting Period for Postal Employees

Section 901 of the Postal Accountability and Enhancement Act, P.L. 109-435, changed the way the FECA three-day waiting period for compensation is applied to employees of the U.S. Postal Service (USPS). This provision requires that postal employees satisfy the three-day waiting period before the continuation of pay period can begin. All other federal employees continue to serve the three-day waiting period after the conclusion of the continuation of pay period and before FECA compensation benefits begin.

This provision was based on a recommendation of the President's Commission on the USPS. The commission's recommendation was part of a larger package of FECA reforms for postal employees intended to reduce the Postal Service's workers' compensation costs. Because of what the commission termed the "unique businesslike charter" of the Postal Service, the commission recommended that the service's workers' compensation system become more in line with the state workers' compensation systems that provide coverage for most private-sector businesses.[26]

Death Gratuity for Federal Employees Killed While Serving Alongside the Armed Forces

American military operations in Iraq and Afghanistan have been supported by an unprecedented number of civilian employees, some of whom are serving in hostile areas alongside the Armed Forces. These deployed civilian employees are covered by FECA, but concerns have been raised about the adequacy of FECA benefits for those injured or killed while serving in areas of combat, especially when compared with the benefits available to members of the Armed Forces from the Departments of Defense and Veterans Affairs.[27]

---

[25] S.Rept. 93-1081, p. 7.

[26] President's Commission on the United States Postal Service, *Embracing the Future: Making the Tough Choices to Preserve Universal Mail Service*, Report of the President's Commission on the United States Postal Service, July 31, 2003, p. 134.

[27] See, for example, U.S. Congress, House Committee on Oversight and Government Reform, Subcommittee on Federal Workforce, Post Office, and the District of Columbia, *A Call to Arms: A Review of Benefits for Deployed Federal Employees*, hearing, 111th Cong., 1st sess., September 16, 2009; and U.S. Congress, Senate Committee on (continued...)

Section 1105 of the National Defense Authorization Act for Fiscal Year 2008, P.L. 110-181, provides for a death gratuity of up to $100,000 to be paid to the survivors of any federal employee, or employee of a non-appropriated fund instrumentality, who "dies of injuries incurred in connection with the employee's service with an Armed Force in a contingency operation." This death gratuity is paid in addition to the regular FECA compensation for survivors, but is offset by any other death gratuities paid by the federal government.

Overview of the FECA Program Today

Statutory and Regulatory Authorities

The FECA program is authorized in statute at 5 U.S.C. Sections 8101 *et seq*. Regulations implementing the FECA are provided at 20 C.F.R. Sections 10.00-10.826. The FECA program is administered by the Department of Labor, Office of Workers' Compensation Programs (OWCP).

Program Financing

Benefits under FECA are paid out of the federal Employees' Compensation Fund. This fund is financed by appropriations from Congress that are used to pay current FECA benefits and that are ultimately reimbursed by federal agencies through the chargeback process.

Each quarter OWCP provides to all federal agencies with employees receiving FECA benefits an estimate of the cost of these benefits to assist these agencies in preparing their budget requests. By August 15 of each year, OWCP sends each agency a statement of their FECA costs for the previous fiscal year. Each agency must include in its next budget request an appropriation to cover its FECA costs for the previous fiscal year. Upon receiving this appropriation, or if a non-appropriated entity of the government, by October 15, the agency must reimburse the Employees' Compensation Fund for the costs of the FECA benefits provided to its employees.

The administrative costs associated with the FECA program are provided to the DOL through the appropriations process. In addition, the USPS and certain other non-appropriated entities of the federal government are required to pay for the "fair share" of the costs of administering benefits for their employees. In 2010, the USPS paid approximately $61 million in FECA administrative costs.[28]

FECA Benefit and Administrative Costs

Table 1 provides data on the costs of providing FECA compensation and medical benefits as well as administrative costs associated with the FECA program. In FY2009, compensation benefits

---

(...continued)

Homeland Security and Governmental Affairs, Subcommittee on Oversight of Government Management, the Federal Workforce, and the District of Columbia, *Deployed Federal Civilians: Advancing Security and Opportunity in Afghanistan*, hearing, 111th Cong., 2nd sess., April 14, 2010.

[28] United States Postal Service, Office of Inspector General, *Postal Service Workers' Compensation Program Audit Report*, Report Number HR-AR-11-007, Washington, DC, September 30, 2011, p. 8.

---

made up 68.7% of the nearly $2.8 billion in total FECA benefits and direct administrative costs made up 5.0% of total program costs.[29]

Table 1. FECA Benefits and Costs, FY2009

	Cost in Thousands of Dollars	Percentage of Total Benefit/Program Costs
Compensation Benefits	1,900,156	68.7
Medical Benefits	863,729	31.3
Total Benefit Costs	*2,763,885*	*100.0*
Direct Administration	146,015	5.0
Total Program Costs	*2,909,900*	*100.0*

Source: Ishita Sengupta, Virginia Reno, and John F. Burton, Jr., *Workers' Compensation: Benefits, Coverage, and Costs, 2009*, National Academy of Social Insurance, Washington, DC, August 2011, p. 79.

Notes: Direct administrative costs are for the administration of FECA program by DOL's OWCP. Indirect administrative costs are for activities, such as investigations or legal support, outside of OWCP.

Employees Covered by FECA

The FECA program covers all civilians employed by the federal government, including employees in the executive, legislative, and judicial branches of the government. Both full-time and part-time workers are covered, as are most volunteers and all persons serving on federal juries. Coverage is also extended to certain groups, including state and local law enforcement officers acting in a federal capacity, federal jurors, Peace Corps volunteers, students participating in Reserve Officer Training Corps programs, and members of the Coast Guard Auxiliary and Civil Air Patrol.

Conditions Covered by FECA

Under FECA, workers' compensation benefits are paid to any covered employee for any disability or death caused by any injury or illness sustained during the employee's work for the federal government. There is no list of covered conditions nor is there a list of conditions that are not covered. However, no injury, illness, or death may be compensated by FECA if the condition was

- caused by the willful misconduct of the employee;

- caused by the employee's intention to bring about the injury or death of himself or another person; or

- proximately caused by the intoxication of the employee.

---

[29] Ishita Sengupta, Virginia Reno, and John F. Burton, Jr., *Workers' Compensation: Benefits, Coverage, and Costs, 2009*, National Academy of Social Insurance, Washington, DC, August 2011, p. 7.,(Hereafter cited as Sengupta et al., 2011.) Direct administrative costs are OWCP's costs of administering the FECA program. Indirect administrative costs are for activities, such as investigations or legal support, outside of OWCP.

In addition, any person convicted of a felony related to the fraudulent application for or receipt of FECA benefits forfeits his or her rights to all FECA benefits for any injury that occurred on or before the date of conviction. The benefits of any person confined in jail, prison, or an institution pursuant to a felony conviction are suspended for the duration of the incarceration and may not be recovered.

FECA Claims Process

All FECA claims are processed and adjudicated by OWCP. Initial decisions on claims are made by OWCP staff based on evidence submitted by the claimant and his or her treating physician. The law also permits OWCP to order a claimant or beneficiary to submit to a medical examination from a doctor contracted to the federal government. An employee dissatisfied with a claims decision may request a hearing before OWCP or an OWCP review of the record of its decision. A final appeal can be made to the Employees' Compensation Appeals Board (ECAB). The decision of the ECAB is final, cannot be appealed, and is not subject to judicial review.

Time Limit for Filing FECA Claims

In general, a claim for disability or death benefits under FECA must be made within three years of the date of the injury or death. In the case of a latent disability, such as a condition caused by exposure to a toxic substance over time, the three-year time limit does not begin until the employee is disabled and is aware, or reasonably should be aware, that the disability was caused by his or her employment.

FECA Compensation Benefits

Continuation of Pay

In the case of a traumatic injury, an employee is eligible for continuation of pay.[30] Continuation of pay is paid by the employing agency and is equal to 100% of the employee's rate of pay at the time of the traumatic injury. Since continuation of pay is considered salary and not compensation, it is taxed and subject to any deductions normally made against the employee's salary. Any lost work time beyond 45 days, or lost time due to a latent condition, is considered either a partial or total disability under FECA.

Employees of the United States Postal Service must satisfy a three-day waiting period before becoming eligible for continuation of pay.

Partial Disability

If an employee is unable to work full-time at his or her previous job, but is able to work either part-time or at a job in a lower pay category, then he or she is considered partially disabled and eligible for the following compensation benefits:

---

[30] Certain groups, including federal jurors, Peace Corps volunteers, and Civil Air Patrol members, are not eligible for continuation of pay.

- if the employee is single, a monthly benefit equal to two-thirds of the difference between the employee's pre-disability and post-disability monthly wage; or

- if the employee has at least one dependent, a monthly benefit equal to 75% of the difference between the employee's pre-disability and post-disability monthly wage.

The compensation benefits paid for partial disability are capped at 75% of the maximum basic pay at rate GS-15 (GS-15, step 10), are not subject to federal taxation, and are subject to an annual cost-of-living adjustment. Benefits are paid for the duration of the disability or the life of the beneficiary.

If an employee's actual wages do not accurately represent his or her true wage-earning capacity, or if he or she has no wages, then his or her partial disability benefit is based on his or her wage-earning capacity as determined by OWCP using a combination of vocational factors and "degree of physical impairment."

Scheduled Benefits

In cases in which an employee suffers a permanent partial disability, such as the loss of a limb, he or she is entitled to a scheduled benefit. The scheduled benefit is in addition to any other partial or total disability benefits received. An employee may receive a scheduled award even if he or she has returned to full-time work.[31] The list of scheduled benefits is provided in the **Appendix** to this report. If an employee suffers a disfigurement of the face, head, or neck that is of such severity that it may limit his or her ability to secure or retain employment, the employee is entitled to up to $3,500 in additional compensation.

Total Disability

If an employee is unable to work at all, then he or she is considered totally disabled and eligible for the following compensation benefits:

- if the employee is single, a monthly benefit equal to two-thirds of the employee's pre-disability monthly wage; or

- if the employee has at least one dependent, a monthly benefit equal to 75% of the employee's pre-disability monthly wage.

The compensation benefits paid for total disability are capped at 75% of the maximum basic pay at rate GS-15 (GS-15, step 10), are not subject to federal taxation, and are subject to an annual cost-of-living adjustment. Benefits are payable until it is determined that the employee is no longer totally disabled and may continue until the employee's death.

---

[31] The list of FECA scheduled benefits are provided in statute at 5 U.S.C. Section 8107(c) and in regulation at 20 C.F.R. Section 10.404(a).

Death

If an employee dies on the job or from a latent condition caused by his or her employment, the employee's survivors are eligible for the following compensation benefits:

- if the employee's spouse has no children, then the spouse is eligible for a monthly benefit equal to 50% of the employee's monthly wage at the time of death; or

- if the employee's spouse has one or more children, then the spouse is eligible for a monthly benefit equal to 45% of the employee's monthly wage at the time of death and each child is eligible for a monthly benefit equal to 15% of the employee's monthly wage at the time of death, up to a maximum family benefit of 75% of the employee's monthly wage at the time of death.

Special rules apply in cases in which an employee dies without a spouse or children or with only children.

If a spouse remarries before the age of 55, then he or she is entitled to a lump-sum payment equal to 24 months of benefits, after which all benefits cease. If a spouse remarries at the age of 55 or older, benefits continue for life. A child's benefits end at the age of 18, or age 23 if the child is still in school. A child's benefits continue for life if the child is disabled and incapable of self-support.

The compensation benefits paid for death are capped at 75% of the maximum basic pay at rate GS-15, are not subject to federal taxation, and are subject to an annual cost-of-living adjustment.

Additional Death Benefits

The personal representative of the deceased employee is entitled to reimbursement, up to $200, of any costs associated with terminating the deceased employee's formal relationship with the federal government. The personal representative of the deceased employee is also entitled to a reimbursement of funeral costs up to $800, and the federal government will pay any costs associated with shipping a body from the place of death to the employee's home. An employee killed while working with the military in a contingency operation is also entitled to a special gratuity payment of up to $100,000 payable to his or her designated survivors.

FECA Medical Benefits

Under FECA, all medical costs—including medical devices, therapies, and medications—associated with the treatment of a covered injury or illness are paid for, in full, by the federal government. A FECA beneficiary is not responsible for any coinsurance or any other costs associated with his or her medical treatment and does not have to use any personal insurance for any covered medical costs. A published fee schedule is used by OWCP to determine the rate or reimbursement paid to medical providers.[32]

---

[32] A copy of the current OWCP medical fee schedule can be found on the Department of Labor website at http://www.dol.gov/owcp/regs/feeschedule/fee.htm.

Generally, a beneficiary may select his or her own medical provider and is reimbursed for the costs associated with transportation to receive medical services. Medical providers must be authorized by OWCP and can have their authorization removed if it is determined that they are violating program rules or are involved in fraud.

A FECA beneficiary who is blind, paralyzed, or otherwise disabled such that he or she needs constant personal attendant care may receive an additional benefit of up to $1,500 per month.

Vocational Rehabilitation

The Secretary of Labor may direct any FECA beneficiary to participate in vocational rehabilitation, the costs of which are paid by the federal government. While participating in vocational rehabilitation, the beneficiary may receive an additional benefit of up to $200 per month. However, any beneficiary who is directed to participate in vocational rehabilitation and fails to do so may have his or her benefit reduced to a level consistent with the increased wage earning capacity that likely would have resulted from participation in vocational rehabilitation.

Coordination with Other Benefits

Coordination with Retirement Benefits for Federal Employees

Most federal employees are covered by either the Civil Service Retirement System (CSRS) or the Federal Employees' Retirement System (FERS).[33] The CSRS covers federal employees initially hired before January 1, 1984. The FERS covers employees hired after that date and CSRS-eligible employees who voluntarily switched to FERS coverage during "open seasons" held in 1986 and 1987. Employees contribute to the cost of the CSRS and FERS through payroll taxes. Both the CSRS and FERS provide for defined benefit pensions for retired and disabled federal employees. The FERS defined benefit pension is smaller than that provided by the CSRS, however, the FERS also provides for participation in the Social Security system and the Thrift Savings Plan (TSP), a federally managed defined contribution plan similar to a 401(k) plan offered to private-sector workers.[34]

While an injured federal employee is receiving FECA benefits and not working, he or she does not make any CSRS or FERS contributions, but does continue to accrue time in service for the purposes of retirement eligibility.[35] Because FECA benefits are not considered earnings under either the Social Security Act or Internal Revenue Code, FECA beneficiaries generally may not contribute to the Social Security system via the payroll tax or to the TSP.

---

[33] Some federal employees, such as Foreign Service Officers or employees of non-appropriated fund instrumentalities, are covered by federal retirement systems other than CSRS or FERS. For additional information on the more than 30 types of federal retirement systems, see U.S. General Accounting Office, *Public Pensions: Summary of Federal Pension Plan Data*, GAO/AIMD-96-6, February 1996. For additional information on the FERS and CSRS, see CRS Report 98-810, *Federal Employees' Retirement System: Benefits and Financing*, by Katelin P. Isaacs.

[34] For additional information on the TSP, see CRS Report RL30387, *Federal Employees' Retirement System: The Role of the Thrift Savings Plan*, by Katelin P. Isaacs.

[35] The only payroll deductions taken from FECA benefits are for Federal Employee Health Benefits (FEHB) and basic, optional, and post-retirement basic life insurance if the employee is enrolled in these programs.

Once a FECA beneficiary becomes eligible for CSRS or FERS retirement benefits, he or she may elect to receive these retirement benefits or remain in the FECA program for the duration of disability. Once this election is made, it may be changed at any time.

That amount of the FERS basic annuity is increased from 1% of the employee's high-three average pay to 2% of the high-three average pay for any period during which the employee was receiving FECA benefits rather than earnings. This provision, enacted in 2003, is designed to partially replace retirement income lost because of the employee's inability to contribute to the Social Security system or the TSP while receiving FECA benefits.[36]

Coordination with Disability Retirement Benefits

Both the CSRS and FERS offer federal employees who are unable to continue working because of disabilities have the option to take a disability retirement annuity before reaching normal retirement age.[37] For the purposes of the CSRS and FERS disability retirement systems, an employee is considered disabled and eligible for an annuity if he or she is unable to perform his or her current federal job and cannot be accommodated with a job at the same rate of pay by his or her employing-agency because of a medical condition that is expected to last at least one year. An employee must have five years of service to qualify for disability retirement benefits under CSRS and 18 month of service under FERS. Generally, the amount of an employee's disability annuity is lower than what the employee would have received had he or she worked until normal retirement age and collected a CSRS or FERS retirement annuity.

As in the cases of a FERS or CSRS retirement annuity, a FECA beneficiary that is also eligible for CSRS or FERS disability retirement benefits may elect to receive these disability retirement benefits or remain in the FECA program for the duration of disability. Once this election is made, it may be changed at any time.

Coordination with Social Security Disability Insurance Benefits

Because FECA is a workers' compensation program, it is covered by the public disability offset provisions of Section 224 of the Social Security Act.[38] If a FECA beneficiary is also receiving Social Security Disability Insurance (SSDI) benefits, then the total amount of the beneficiary's monthly SSDI benefit, all SSDI benefits paid to his or her spouse or dependents, and his or her FECA benefit cannot exceed 80% of his or her average monthly wage at the time of his or her disability.[39] The FECA beneficiary's SSDI benefits, or the benefits for his or her spouse or dependents, are reduced until the 80% threshold is reached.

---

[36] P.L. 108-92.

[37] For additional information on disability retirement under CSRS and FERS, see CRS Report RS22838, *Disability Retirement for Federal Employees*, by Katelin P. Isaacs.

[38] 42 U.S.C. §424a.

[39] For additional information on the SSDI program, see CRS Report RL32279, *Primer on Disability Benefits: Social Security Disability Insurance (SSDI) and Supplemental Security Income (SSI)*, by Umar Moulta-Ali.

Coordination with Social Security Retirement Benefits

Federal employees covered by the FERS system are also covered by the Social Security system for their periods of federal employment. If a federal employee covered by FERS is entitled to both FECA and Social Security retirement benefits, the amount of his or her monthly FECA benefit is reduced by the amount of his or her Social Security retirement benefit attributable to his or her federal service.

Selected Current Issues Facing the FECA Program

In the 112th Congress, the House and Senate have held hearings that have addressed several issues facing the FECA program, including the cost of FECA benefits for postal workers, the proper role of FECA compensation benefits for injured workers as they age, and comparisons between the FECA program and state workers' compensation programs that cover the majority of private-sector and state and local government workers in the country.[40]

In addition, as part of larger U.S. Postal Service (USPS) reform legislation, the House Committee on Oversight and Government Reform reported legislation (H.R. 2309) that would make changes to the FECA program as it applies to postal workers. The Senate passed legislation (S. 1789) that would make significant reforms to the FECA program for all federal employees. The main vehicle for FECA program reform in the House is H.R. 2465, which was passed by the House and which would make changes to the FECA program for all federal employees.

> **FECA Legislation Reported in the 112th Congress**
> - Postal Reform Act of 2001, H.R. 2309
>
> **FECA Legislation Passed by the House of Representatives in the 112th Congress**
> - Federal Workers' Compensation Modernization and Improvement Act, H.R. 2465
>
> **FECA Legislation Passed by the Senate in the 112th Congress**
> - 21st Century Postal Act of 2011, S. 1789

FECA and the U.S. Postal Service

The USPS and its employees make up the largest component of the FECA program, and postal workers are injured on the job at rates disproportionate to the rest of the federal government. As shown in **Table 2**, although postal workers make up 21.2% of the federal workforce, they are responsible for 37.4% of injuries, illnesses, and fatalities that resulted in FECA cases in FY2010.[41]

---

[40] U.S. Congress, House Committee on Oversight and Government Reform, Subcommittee on Federal Workforce, U.S. Postal Service, and Labor Policy, *FECA: A Fair Approach*, 112th Cong., 1st sess., April 13, 2011; U.S. Congress, House Committee on Education and the Workforce, Subcommittee on Workforce Protections, *Reviewing Workers' Compensation for Federal Employees*, 112th Cong., 1st sess., May 12, 2011; and U.S. Congress, Senate Committee on Homeland Security and Governmental Affairs, Subcommittee on Oversight of Government Management, the Federal Workforce, and the District of Columbia, *Examining the Federal Workers' Compensation Program for Injured Employees*, 112th Cong., 1st sess., July 26, 2011.

[41] Department of Labor, Occupational Safety and Health Administration, *Federal Injury and Illness Statistics for Fiscal Year 2010*, http://www.osha.gov/dep/fap/statistics/fedprgms_stats10_final.html#footnote4a.

The most significant area in which the experience of the USPS with the FECA program differs from that of the rest of the government is in the severity and duration of injuries and illnesses that result in FECA cases. As shown in **Table 3**, in FY2010, injuries and illnesses to postal workers resulted in 218.7 lost production days per 100 employees, compared with 77.4 days for the entire federal government and 34.8 days for non-postal federal entities.[42] This means that for every one of the nearly 600,000 postal workers, more than two days of work were lost due to injuries, illnesses, or fatalities and that an estimated total of 1,298,750 production days, or 4,995 work years at the USPS were lost in FY2010 due to injuries, illnesses, and fatalities.[43]

Table 2. FECA Cases, FY2010

Category	Employees[a]		FECA Cases[b]		
	Total	Percentage	Total	Percentage	Per 100 Employees
Federal Government	2,804,206	100.0	108,587	100.0	3.9
U.S. Postal Service	593,850	21.2	40,588	37.4	6.8
Federal Government, excluding U.S. Postal Service	2,210,356	78.8	67,996	62.6	3.1

Source: Congressional Research Service (CRS) table with data taken from Department of Labor, Occupational Safety and Health Administration, *Federal Injury and Illness Statistics for Fiscal Year 2010*, http://www.osha.gov/dep/fap/statistics/fedprgms_stats10_final.html#footnote4a.

Note: Numbers may not add due to rounding and the number of federal employees calculated at different times during the year.

a.   As of June 2010.

b.   Includes all new injury, illness, and fatality cases submitted to FECA, less any denied claims.

The USPS was the only federal entity with more than 200 lost production days per 100 employees in FY2010, and in FY2010 the only two other entities that had at least 150 lost production days were the Armed Forces Retirement Home and the International Boundary and Water Commission, small entities with approximately 250 employees each. The USPS in FY2010 was responsible for 60% of the total number of lost production days by the entire federal government.

Given the disproportionate number of injuries and lost production days attributed to the USPS, it is not surprising that benefits for postal workers make up a disproportionate share of the total costs of the FECA program. In chargeback year 2009, the FECA program paid approximately

---

[42]   Department of Labor, Office of Workers' Compensation Programs, *FY2010 End of Year LPD Report for All Government*, http://www.dol.gov/owcp/dfec/share/lpd/FY20104thQtr/AllGovernment.htm.

[43]   The total number of lost production days is calculated based on June 2010 employment data compiled by the Occupational Safety and Health Administration (OSHA) from various sources and posted on its website at http://www.osha.gov/dep/fap/statistics/fedprgms_stats10_final.html#footnote1 and on end-of-fiscal year injury data reported by the Department of Labor on its website at http://www.dol.gov/owcp/dfec/share/lpd/FY20104thQtr/AllGovernment.htm. Because the number of federal employees fluctuates throughout the year, and because no one agency of the federal government collects data on employment in the executive, legislative, and judicial branches of the government, the calculated number of total lost production days must be treated as an estimate. The estimated number of lost work years is calculated based on 260 work days in a work year.

$2.7 billion in total benefits, with nearly $1.1 billion in benefits, or 40% of total benefits, being paid for claims by postal workers.[44]

As discussed earlier in this report, in 2006, with the enactment of P.L. 109-435, Congress changed the application of the three-day waiting period for postal workers with traumatic injuries with the goal of reducing FECA costs to the USPS. Under this provision, postal workers now must satisfy the three-day FECA waiting period before the beginning of the continuation of pay period, rather than after this period and before receiving FECA compensation.

Table 3. Lost Time FECA Cases and Lost Production Days due to Injuries, Illnesses, and Deaths, FY2010

Category	Lost Time Cases			Lost Production Days Per 100 Employees
	Total	Percentage	Per 100 Employees	
Federal Government	47,226	100.0	1.68	77.4
U.S. Postal Service	15,311	32.4	2.58	218.7
Federal Government, excluding U.S. Postal Service	31,915	67.6	1.44	34.8

Source: The Congressional Research Service (CRS) with data taken from Department of Labor, Occupational Safety and Health Administration, Federal Injury and Illness Statistics for Fiscal Year 2010, http://www.osha.gov/dep/fap/statistics/fedprgms_stats10_final.html#footnote4a; and Department of Labor, Office of Workers' Compensation Programs, FY2010 End of Year LPD Report for All Government, http://www.dol.gov/owcp/dfec/share/lpd/FY20104thQtr/AllGovernment.htm.

Note: Numbers may not add due to rounding and the number of federal employees calculated at different times during the year.

Legislative Activity

The House postal reform legislation is the only one of the three active bills to directly address the FECA program for postal workers. Specifically, H.R. 2309 would require the U.S. Postal Service to design and implement a new workers' compensation system for its employees that would prohibit the payment of augmented compensation for dependents and require some form of transition to or coordination with retirement benefits. This requirement would only go into effect, however, if the Postal Service Financial Responsibility and Management Assistance Authority created by the legislation determines that the financial condition of the USPS warrants such a change.

FECA and Retirement Age

Both FECA compensation and medical benefits are payable for the duration of a person's disability. There is no maximum duration of benefits and no maximum age at which benefits must be terminated. Beneficiaries who are eligible for CSRS or FERS retirement or disability annuities may chose to remain in the FECA program. Given the level of benefits, which can be as high as

---

[44] Department of Labor, Office of Workers' Compensation Programs, *Annual Report to Congress: FY2009*, Washington, DC, April 27, 2011, p. 11. A chargeback year runs from July 1 to June 30.

75% of a worker's pre-disability wage; the annual cost-of-living adjustment to benefits; and the fact that FECA benefits are not taxed, in some cases the monthly FECA benefit is higher than what would be paid by a CSRS or FERS annuity. In addition, because FECA beneficiaries who are not working do not pay into either the Social Security system or the TSP, they may be unable to rely on these programs as a significant source of retirement income.

The Department of Labor reports that although less than 2% of new injury cases stay on the FECA rolls for more than two years, approximately 45,000 cases currently receive long-term disability benefits and 15,000, or one-third of these cases involve beneficiaries aged 66 or older.[45] The U.S. Postal Service Office of Inspector General reports that the FECA rolls include 9,554 postal workers aged 55 or older; 3,389 aged 65 or older; and 928 aged 80 or older, including one aged 99.[46]

The provision of FECA compensation benefits to workers after retirement age has changed during the history of the FECA program. Although FECA benefits have always been paid for the duration of disability, between 1949 and 1974, the administrator of the FECA program was required to review the amount of benefits paid to each beneficiary at the age of 70 and was authorized to reduce the amount of such benefits if it was determined that the beneficiary's wage-earning capacity had been reduced by his or her age, independent of his or her disability. This provision was repealed in 1974 with the Senate Committee on Labor and Public Welfare calling the reduction of benefits at the age of 70 "discriminatory."[47]

Policy Considerations

The question of whether FECA benefits should continue past retirement age depends somewhat on the intent of these benefits. If FECA disability benefits are intended solely to replace income lost by a worker because of an injury or illness, then one can reasonably argue that these benefits should stop at retirement age, when the worker would likely voluntarily stop working on his or her own, and thus no longer have wages to be replaced. It could be argued that the provision of FECA benefits for wage loss is analogous to the SSDI program, which stops paying benefits when a disabled beneficiary reaches retirement age. However, SSDI benefits automatically convert to Social Security retirement benefits at retirement age.

However, if FECA disability benefits are intended to provide some relief to the worker beyond wage replacement, such as providing additional money that might have been paid by an at-fault employer through the tort system or guaranteeing a certain minimum standard of living for a disabled worker, then stopping benefits at any age while the disability continues would violate this intent and deprive the beneficiary of deserved benefits.

Currently, 14 states and the District of Columbia place limitations on the duration of permanent total disability benefits under their workers' compensation systems. These limitations are in the

---

[45] U.S. Congress, Senate Committee on Homeland Security and Governmental Affairs, Subcommittee on Oversight of Government Management, the Federal Workforce, and the District of Columbia, *Examining the Federal Workers' Compensation Program for Injured Employees*, 112th Cong., 1st sess., July 26, 2011, (statement of Gary Steinberg, Acting Director, Office of Workers' Compensation Programs).

[46] U.S. Postal Service Office of Inspector General, *Postal Service Workers' Compensation Program: Audit Report*, Report Number HR-AR-11-007, September 30, 2011, p. 1.

[47] S. Rept. 93-1081, p. 7.

form of a maximum number of weeks benefits may be paid, a termination of benefits at retirement or some other age, or a combination of both.[48] Federal workers' compensation benefits paid through the Longshore and Harbor Workers' Compensation Act are paid for the duration of disability or the life of the beneficiary.

Legislative Activity

The legislation in the Senate includes provisions that would limit benefits to persons over the retirement age. Specifically, S. 1789 would reduce the amount of the basic FECA disability benefit to 50% of a workers' pre-disability wage when he or she reaches the full-retirement age for Social Security.[49] Certain current beneficiaries with permanent total disabilities would not be affected by this provision.

In the House, FECA reform legislation (H.R. 2465) does not include any provisions that would change FECA benefit amounts for beneficiaries at retirement age. However, in July 2011, the chairman and ranking Member of the House Education and Workforce Committee and the Subcommittee on Workforce Protections wrote a letter to the comptroller general requesting that the Government Accountability Office (GAO) examine several policy proposals regarding the FECA program, including a proposal to reduce the FECA benefits of persons over the Social Security full-retirement age to 50% of the pre-disability wage.[50]

FECA Benefit Generosity

In general, FECA disability benefits are more generous than those offered by state workers' compensation systems. For workers with traumatic injuries, FECA offers continuation of pay, at full salary, for the first 45 days. No state system currently provides any type of continuation of pay, absent the use of some form of sick or personal leave. Disability benefits under FECA are adjusted annually to reflect changes in the cost of living, a provision generally not found in state systems.

The maximum FECA benefit is based on 75% of the GS-15, Step 10 pay rate, without any locality adjustments whereas state maximums are generally based on state average wages or the worker's own pre-disability wage. For 2011, the annual salary at GS-15, Step 10, is $129,517, whereas the average federal salary for the executive branch in March 2011 was $74,915.[51] Thus, the maximum FECA benefit under the current system is higher than it would be if the FECA system based its maximum benefit level on average wages as is the case in the majority of the states.

---

[48] Sengupta, et al., 2011, pp. 86-95.

[49] For additional information on the Social Security retirement age, see CRS Report R41962, *Fact Sheet: The Social Security Retirement Age*, by Alison M. Shelton.

[50] This letter is available on the website of the House Committee on Education and the Workforce at http://edworkforce.house.gov/UploadedFiles/GAO_FECA_July_2011.pdf.

[51] Information on the GS-15 salary rate taken from the website of the Office of Personnel Management (OPM) at http://www.opm.gov/oca/11tables/html/gs.asp. Information on average federal salary taken form the OPM FedScope system online at http://www.fedscope.opm.gov/.

The FECA basic benefit rate for total disability is two-thirds of the worker's pre-disability wage. Currently, 36 states and the District of Columbia have total disability benefit rates that are set at this level.[52] Benefits under the federal Longshore and Harbor Workers' Compensation Act are also set at two-thirds of the pre-disability wage. New Hampshire's benefit rate is 60% of the worker's pre-disability wage.

Currently, four states have total disability benefit rates that are based on pre-disability or average wages and that exceed the two-thirds standard. In New Jersey and Oklahoma, benefits are paid at 70% of the worker's wage at the time of injury whereas benefits in Texas are based on 75% of the worker's average wage. In Ohio, benefits are paid at 72% of the pre-disability wage for the first 12 weeks, then are reduced to the standard two-thirds rate.

Six states—Alaska, Connecticut, Iowa, Maine, Michigan, and Rhode Island—base benefits on net, rather than gross wages. It is generally not possible to compare these benefits to FECA benefits because of differences in tax rates that affect net income. Three states—Georgia, Pennsylvania, and Washington—have systems in which there is no direct comparison to the FECA total disability benefit rate.

Because of the augmented compensation provision of the FECA program, beneficiaries with dependents, including spouses, may receive total disability benefits at a rate of 75% of their pre-disability wages. No state pays augmented compensation for dependents, and the 75% benefit rate is higher than that paid by any comparable state workers' compensation system. Currently, more than 70% of FECA beneficiaries are receiving augmented compensation, and thus benefits at the rate of 75% of their pre-disability wages.[53]

One indication of the benefit generosity of the FECA program compared with state workers' compensation programs is the amount of disability benefits paid as a percentage of total program benefits. In 2009, disability benefits made up 49.1% of the total costs of benefits paid by state workers' compensation programs and 70.7% of total benefits paid by the FECA program.[54] Assuming that the types of injuries faced by federal employees and workers in the private and non-federal public sectors are not significantly different and that medical costs are also similar, this difference can be attributed to the generosity of FECA disability benefits, especially for higher-wage workers, compared with those offered by state workers' compensation systems.[55]

Legislative Activity

H.R. 2465 does not include provisions that would reduce the overall generosity of FECA benefits. Rather, H.R. 2465 would increase the continuation of pay period for federal employees serving in areas of armed conflict and increase funeral and disfigurement benefits. S. 1789 would eliminate

---

[52] Sengupta et al., 2011, pp. 86-95.

[53] U.S. Congress, Senate Committee on Homeland Security and Governmental Affairs, Subcommittee on Oversight of Government Management, the Federal Workforce, and the District of Columbia, *Examining the Federal Workers' Compensation Program for Injured Employees*, 112th Cong., 1st sess., July 26, 2011 (statement of Gary Steinberg, Acting Director, Office of Workers' Compensation Programs).

[54] Sengupta et al., 2011, pp. 24-25.

[55] This conclusion is supported by Sengupta et al. who state "The share of benefits for medical care is lower than in most state programs because federal cash benefits, particularly for higher-wage workers, replace a larger share of pre-injury wages than is the case in most state programs" (Sengupta et al., 2011, p. 78).

augmented compensation except in certain cases of existing totally disabled beneficiaries, while increasing funeral and disfigurement benefits. The new U.S. Postal Service workers' compensation program that could be created under the provisions of H.R. 2309 would be prohibited from paying augmented compensation for dependents.

Program Administration

Insurance

The administration of state workers' compensation systems and the provision of insurance and benefits differs significantly from the FECA program. The FECA program does not involve any form of private insurance or private third-party administration of claims or benefits. Essentially, each federal entity acts like a self-insured employer with OWCP in the role of claims and benefit manager.

State workers' compensation benefits are generally provided by private insurance, state insurance funds, or through self insurance. All but four states—North Dakota, Ohio, Washington, and Wyoming—allow for private insurance. In Ohio and Washington, employers may either purchase insurance form the state fund or self-insure, whereas employers in North Dakota and Wyoming may not self-insure and must purchase coverage from the state fund. In 22 states, employers may purchase insurance from either a state fund or private carriers. All states except North Dakota and Wyoming allow self-insurance. Under the federal Longshore and Harbor Workers' Compensation Act, employers may purchase private insurance or self-insure.

Private insurance pays the majority of state workers' compensation benefits. In 2009, private insurers paid 55.6% of total state workers' compensation benefits whereas state funds paid 18.5% and self-insured firms paid 25.9%.[56] Thus, nearly three-quarters of all state workers' compensation benefits are paid through a system of third-party insurance rather than through the self-insurance model used by the FECA program.

Neither FECA reform legislation (H.R. 2465) nor postal reform legislation (S. 1789) would change the administration of FECA benefits or permit any type of private or third-party insurance. However, the postal reform legislation (H.R. 2309) would give broad discretion to the USPS to establish its own workers' compensation program, which could include private or third-party insurance.

Settlements

In 43 states and the District of Columbia, workers' compensation insurers or self-insured firms may enter into compromise and release settlements with claimants.[57] In these settlements, the insurer or firm agrees to pay the claimant lump-sum or periodic payment in exchange for being released from all future obligations under the claim. Compromise and release settlements are commonly used to avoid protracted disputes or litigation involving claims and are common in

---

[56] Sengupta et al., 2011, pp. 24-25.

[57] Peter S. Barth, *Compromise and Release Settlements in Workers' Compensation: Final Report*, W.E. Upjohn Institute for Employment Research, report prepared for the State of Washington, Department of Labor and Industries, December 21, 2010, pp. 44-45, http://research.upjohn.org/reports/178/.

cases with potential for long-term payment of benefits. To accept a compromise and release settlement, the claimant generally must agree to forgo future benefits, which may be higher over his or her lifetime, in exchange for immediate payment. Insurers or firms must agree to forgo the possibility of lower future payments because of successfully controverting parts of a claim or the death, medical improvement, or return to work of the claimant, in exchange for clearing a claim off of their books with an immediate payment.

A 2010 study by the W.E. Upjohn Institute for Employment Research found that for 14 large states (California, Florida, Iowa, Illinois, Indiana, Louisiana, Massachusetts, Maryland, Michigan, North Carolina, Pennsylvania, Tennessee, Texas, and Wisconsin), for claims that originated between October 2003 and September 2004, and that had at least seven days of total lost work time, by March 2007, a median of 19% of these cases had been settled.[58]

Federal law does not provide for the settlement of FECA claims. Thus, the FECA program and FECA claimants are not able to take advantage of a tool used in approximately one-fifth of claims with the potential for long-term benefits, including the types of claims that are likely to result in beneficiaries receiving benefits well after retirement age.

Legislative Activity

The FECA reform legislation (H.R. 2465 and S. 1789) do not contain provisions that would permit the use of compromise and release settlements in the FECA program. Although the postal reform legislation (H.R. 2309) does not directly address the use of settlements, the broad authority given the USPS to create its own workers' compensation program could result in the use of settlements within that new program.

---

[58] Ibid., p. 43.

Appendix. FECA Scheduled Benefits

Table A-1. FECA Scheduled Benefits for Partial Disability Compensation

Loss of Use of Body System	Number of Weeks of Compensation
Scheduled benefits provided by statute [5 U.S.C. §8107(c)]	
Arm	312
Leg	288
Hand	244
Foot	205
Eye	106
Thumb	75
First finger	46
Great toe	38
Second finger	30
Third finger	25
Toe other than great toe	16
Fourth finger	15
Loss of hearing in one ear	52
Loss of hearing in both ears	200
Scheduled benefits provided by regulation [20 C.F.R. §10.404(a)]	
Breast	52
Kidney	156
Larynx	160
Lung	156
Penis	205
Testicle	52
Tongue	160
Ovary	52
Uterus or cervix	52
Vulva or vagina	52

Source: The Congressional Research Service.

Notes: Compensation is equal to two-thirds of the pre-disability wage of a single employee or 75% of the pre-disability wage of an employee with dependents for the number of weeks indicated.

Author Contact Information

Scott Szymendera
Analyst in Disability Policy
sszymendera@crs.loc.gov, 7-0014

www.ingramcontent.com/pod-product-compliance
Lightning Source LLC
Chambersburg PA
CBHW081246170526
45165CB00009B/3220